Available from A Tribe of Two Press:

Three Learning Stories by
Paula Underwood:

Who Speaks for Wolf
Winter White and Summer Gold
Many Circles, Many Paths

And to be used with them:

Three Strands in the Braid: A Guide
for Enablers of Learning

Also now available:

The Walking People:
A Native American Oral History

Who Speaks for Wolf

Who Speaks for Wolf

A NATIVE AMERICAN LEARNING STORY

By Paula Underwood
Art by Frank Howell

A Tribe of Two Press • San Anselmo • 1991

First edition, 1983, enabled by the Meredith Slobod Crist
Memorial Fund, Kerrville, Texas, and by the Overseas Edu-
cation Fund, Washington, DC; published as a memorial to
Meredith Slobod Crist:
> Bright Comet
> Briefly seen
> Illuminating life
> With a glad vision.

Second edition, 1991, A Tribe of Two Press
New Material © 1991 by Paula Underwood
Library of Congress Catalog Card #91-65522
ISBN 1-879678-01-2

Edited by Jeanne Lamar Slobod
Designed by Robert J. Helberg

Produced by AMS Publications, Georgetown, Texas

For information, contact:
A Tribe of Two Press
PO Box 216
San Anselmo, California 94979
(415) 457-6548

Dedicated to my Grandfather

Oliver Perry Underwood — Grey Wolf Walking
Whose wise choice shows us the path

Grey Wolf Walking

Pacing the silent forest
Searching out Earth wisdom
Grey Wolf looks up
And sings to the night

Echoes of such singing
Brush against treetops
Touch distant stars
And the night remembers

Acknowledgements

"The Beauty of the Learning Way," my Father said, "can be seen by many. It remains only to give them the chance to see."

In the slow process of sharing this Learning Story, I have learned how accurate my Father was. Many have seen the Beauty of this Learning Way — and I acknowledge them.

Here I acknowledge my family — my Father, my Grandfather, his Grandmother — and celebrate their wisdom in preserving this Path.

Here, I acknowledge my friend and editor, Jeanne Lamar Slobod, who was certain this Way must be shared and has bent her mind, her heart, and her hand to enable.

Here I acknowledge those who have been drawn together through this Story — La Donna Harris who helps me learn about today, Jackie Wasilewski who helps work through the cultural variations, Val Taylor who has a particular affinity for Wolf, Sarah Ann Robertson who consults and consoles, Bob Helberg who always encourages the next step.

Here I acknowledge all the old friends, the new friends who have each in their own way joined me in this task of sharing — each of them adds in some way to the breadth of human understanding.

Here I acknowledge each of you who choose a Learning Story for the Beauty of the Learning Way.

A grateful heart comes singing.

Introduction

Who Speaks for Wolf is truly a Learning Story. It has been designed over many generations to encourage people to think, to understand, to consider, to remember. When I learned this Telling from my Father, along with many other things, I knew I had not completed my task. There was another learning in store! How and where to share.

For many years I have been experimenting with the possibilities of sharing all the learnings that my family has preserved from an ancient and effective past. As I struggled, many of my friends took an interest in this process and added their labor to my own — volunteering to type, to hold group readings followed by discussion, to contact people, to encourage, to ease the path.

When an opportunity came to publish, we chose the first of the Three Learning Stories, *Who Speaks for Wolf*, and were amazed at the response.

Before the ink was dry, people in the Austin, Texas, Independent School District had asked to use this ancient Learning Story in a Pilot Program in one of their schools.

At the same time, unbeknownst to us, a copy had found its way into the hands of a Virginia librarian, Nancy Strachan, who immediately submitted it to the Virginia Library Association's award committee. That year *Who Speaks for Wolf* won the VLA's Thomas Jefferson Cup, a nationwide award for quality writing in the field of American history suitable for children and young adults. I find it profoundly appropriate that a Learning Story should receive an award named after such a learning man!

Teachers in the Austin Pilot Project were so enthusiastic

and so sure that there was more to learn, that their questions grew into a Teacher's Guide, which we then tested in more than 60 schools nationwide.

Then, both the Texas Council on the Humanities and the U.S. Department of Education declared *Wolf* and the Teacher's Guide an Exemplary Program. We call this educational program "The Past Is Prologue." Under this title it is listed in the catalogue of "Educational Programs That Work."

By now, *Who Speaks for Wolf* is used in schools at all age levels, in environmental teaching, in decision-making classes, in corporate training. It is used in counseling teenagers and victims of abuse. It is used in values clarification and in training for peace.

In 1990 the West Institute included "The Past Is Prologue" educational program in one of its summer seminars. Fourteen Leader Teachers spent two weeks learning more and more about this learning process. Each of them received one of the last remaining copies of the first edition of *Wolf* and the Teacher's Guide. We were sold out. Yet these teachers needed classroom copies — and we had collected a sizeable stack of orders we could not fill.

For all of these reasons we have formed A Tribe of Two Press into a business — again with much help from friends. The purpose of A Tribe of Two Press is to enable us to share all the learnings handed down in this family from generation to generation.

For all these reasons we now publish this paperback edition of *Who Speaks for Wolf* for the use of every learner — old or young, in class or at home, in universities and in businesses. It will soon be joined by the other two Learning Stories. At the same time we are issuing *Three Strands in the Braid: A Guide for Enablers of Learning*, the third edition of this work designed for use in each and every learning circumstance, from kindergarten to graduate school, from counseling to corporations.

For all of these reasons work is ongoing to develop additional ways in which to share more and more elements in this gathered Learning Way.

In 1993 the long-awaited consensual Oral History, *The Walking People*, was published in cooperation with the Institute of Noetic Sciences. All Earth's children can now share this 840-page telling of a continuous and purposeful Native American people who cared that the children's children might remember . . and Learn.

Welcome to the growing number of people who choose to learn from such possibilities.

Now,
Kind thoughts come,

Paula Underwood
Turtle Woman Singing

13

Who Speaks for Wolf

Almost at the edge of the circle of light cast by Central Fire — Wolf was standing. His eyes reflected the fire's warmth with a colder light. Wolf stood there, staring at the fire.

A boy of eight winters was watching Wolf — as immobile as Wolf — as fascinated. Finally, the boy turned to Grandfather, warming his old bones from winter's first chill.

"Why does Wolf stand there and only watch the fire?"

"Why do you?" Grandfather replied.

And then the boy remembered that he had sat there, ever since the fire was lit, watching the flames — until Wolf came. Now, instead, he watched Wolf. He saw that it was because Wolf was so different from him, yet also watched the fire, and that there seemed no fear in Wolf. It was this the boy did not understand.

Beyond where Wolf was standing there was a hill — still so close to the Central Fire that the boy was surprised to see the dim outline of another Wolf face. This one was looking at the moon.

Moon-Looking-Wolf began to sing her song. More and more joined her until at last even Wolf-Looks-at-Fire chortled in his throat the beginnings of a song. They sang for the Moon, and for each other, and for any who might listen. They sang of how Earth was a good place to be, of how much beauty surrounds us, and of how all this is sometimes most easily seen in Moon and Fire.

The boy listened — and wanted to do nothing else with his life but listen to Wolf singing.

After a long and particularly beautiful song, Moon-Looking-Wolf quieted, and one by one her brothers joined her in silence, until even the most distant —crying "I am here! Don't forget me!" — made space for the night and watched — and waited. Wolf-Looks-at-Fire turned and left the clearing, joining his brothers near the hill.

But I still don't understand," the boy continued. "Why does Wolf look at Fire? Why does he feel at home so close to our living space? Why does Wolf Woman begin her song on a hill so close to us who are not Wolf?"

"We have known each other for a long time," the old man answered. "We have learned to live with one another."

The boy still looked puzzled. Within himself he saw only the edges of understanding.

Grandfather was silent for a time — and then began at last the slow cadences of a chant. The boy knew with satisfaction that soon he would understand — would know Wolf better than before — would learn how it had been between us.

LONG AGO . . . LONG AGO . . . LONG AGO . . .

Grandfather chanted, the rhythm taking its place with Wolf's song as something appropriate for the forest.

LONG AGO
  Our People grew in number so that where we were
    was no longer enough
  Many young men
    were sent out from among us
      to seek a new place
        where the People might be who-they-were
  They searched
    and they returned
      each with a place selected
      each determined his place was best

AND SO IT WAS
  That the People had a decision to make:
    which of the many was most appropriate

NOW, AT THAT TIME
  There was one among the People
    to whom Wolf was brother
  He was so much Wolf's brother
    that he would sing their song to them
      and they would answer him
  He was so much Wolf's brother
    that their young
      would sometimes follow him through the forest
      and it seemed they meant to learn from him

SO IT WAS, AT THIS TIME
  That the People gave That One a special name
  They called him WOLF'S BROTHER
    and if any sought to learn about Wolf
    if any were curious
      or wanted to learn to sing Wolf's song
        they would sit beside him
          and describe their curiosity
            hoping for a reply

"Has it been since that time that we sing to Wolf?" the boy asked eagerly. "Was it he who taught us how?" He clapped his hands over his mouth to stop the tumble of words. He knew he had interrupted Grandfather's Song.

The old man smiled, and the crinkles around his eyes spoke of other boys — and other times.

"Yes, even he!" he answered. "For since that time it has pleased many of our people to sing to Wolf and to learn to understand him."

Encouraged, the boy asked, "And ever since our hunters go to learn to sing to Wolf?"

"Many people go, not only hunters. Many people go, not only men," Grandfather chided. "For was it not Wolf Woman who began the song tonight? Would it then be appropriate if only the men among us replied?"

The boy looked crestfallen. He wanted so much to be a hunter — to learn Wolf's song, but he knew there was wisdom in Grandfather's words. Not only hunters learn from Wolf.

"But you have led me down a different path," the Old One was saying. "It would please me to finish my first song."

The boy settled back and waited to learn.

AS I HAVE SAID
   The people sought a new place in the forest
   They listened closely to each of the young men
      as they spoke of hills and trees
         of clearings and running water
         of deer and squirrel and berries
   They listened to hear which place
      might be drier in rain
      more protected in winter
      and where our Three Sisters
         Corn, Beans, and Squash
            might find a place to their liking
   They listened
      and they chose

Before they chose
   they listened to each young man
Before they chose
   they listened to each among them
      he who understood the flow of waters
      she who understood Long House construction
      he who understood the storms of winter
      she who understood Three Sisters
   to each of these they listened
      until they reached agreement
      and the Eldest among them
         finally rose and said:
            "SO BE IT —
               FOR SO IT IS"

25

"BUT WAIT"
 Someone cautioned —
  "Where is Wolf's Brother?
   WHO, THEN, SPEAKS FOR WOLF?"

BUT
 THE PEOPLE·WERE DECIDED
  and their mind was firm
  and the first people were sent
   to choose a site for the first Long House
   to clear a space for our Three Sisters
   to mold the land so that water
    would run away from our dwelling
     so that all would be secure within

AND THEN WOLF'S BROTHER RETURNED
    He asked about the New Place
        and said at once that we must choose another
        "You have chosen the Center Place
          for a great community of Wolf"
    But we answered him
        that many had already gone
        and that it could not wisely be changed
        and that surely Wolf could make way for us
          as we sometimes make way for Wolf
    But Wolf's Brother counseled —
        "I think that you will find
          that it is too small a place for both
          and that it will require more work then —
            than change would presently require"

BUT
    THE PEOPLE CLOSED THEIR EARS
    and would not reconsider
    When the New Place was ready
        all the People rose up as one
        and took those things they found of value
        and looked at last upon their new home

NOW CONSIDER HOW IT WAS FOR THEM
  This New Place
    had cool summers and winter protection
    and fast-moving streams
    and forests around us
      filled with deer and squirrel
    there was room even for our Three Beloved Sisters

AND THE PEOPLE SAW THAT THIS WAS GOOD
  AND DID NOT SEE
    WOLF WATCHING FROM THE SHADOWS!

BUT AS TIME PASSED
  They began to see —
    for someone would bring deer or squirrel
      and hang him from a tree
      and go for something to contain the meat
      but would return
        to find nothing hanging from the tree
        AND WOLF BEYOND

AT FIRST
  This seemed to us an appropriate exchange —
    some food for a place to live

BUT

    It soon became apparent that it was more than this —
        for Wolf would sometimes walk between the dwellings
            that we had fashioned for ourselves
                and the women grew concerned
                    for the safety of the little ones
  Thinking of this
      they devised for a while an agreement with Wolf
        whereby the women would gather together
            at the edge of our village
            and put out food for Wolf and his brothers

BUT IT WAS SOON APPARENT

  That this meant too much food
    and also Wolf grew bolder
      coming in to look for food
        so that it was worse than before
WE HAD NO WISH TO TAME WOLF

AND SO

  Hearing the wailing of the women
    the men devised a system
      whereby some ones among them
        were always alert to drive off Wolf

AND WOLF WAS SOON HIS OLD UNTAMED SELF

BUT
  They soon discovered
    that this required so much energy
      that there was little left for winter preparations
      and the Long Cold began to look longer and colder
      with each passing day

THEN
The men counseled together
to choose a different course

THEY SAW
That neither providing Wolf with food
nor driving him off
gave the People a life that was pleasing

THEY SAW
That Wolf and the People
could not live comfortably together
in such a small space

THEY SAW
That it was possible
to hunt down this Wolf People
until they were no more

BUT THEY ALSO SAW
   That this would require much energy over many years

THEY SAW, TOO,
   That such a task would change the People:
      they would become Wolf Killers
   A People who took life only to sustain their own
      would become a People who took life
         rather than move a little

IT DID NOT SEEM TO THEM
   THAT THEY WANTED TO BECOME SUCH A PEOPLE

AT LAST
   One of the Eldest of the People
      spoke what was in every mind:
      "It would seem
         that Wolf's Brother's vision
            was sharper than our own
   To live here indeed requires more work now
      than change would have made necessary"

Grandfather paused, making his knee a drum on which to maintain the rhythm of the chant, and then went on.

NOW THIS WOULD BE A SIMPLE TELLING
  OF A PEOPLE WHO DECIDED TO MOVE
    ONCE WINTER WAS PAST

EXCEPT
  THAT FROM THIS
    THE PEOPLE LEARNED A GREAT LESSON

IT IS A LESSON
  WE HAVE NEVER FORGOTTEN

FOR

At the end of their Council

one of the Eldest rose again and said:

"Let us learn from this

so that not again

need the People build only to move

Let us not again think we will gain energy

only to lose more than we gain

We have learned to choose a place

where winter storms are less

rather than rebuild

We have learned to choose a place

where water does not stand

rather than sustain sickness

LET US NOW LEARN TO CONSIDER WOLF!"

36

AND SO IT WAS
 That the People devised among themselves
  a way of asking each other questions
   whenever a decision was to be made
    on a New Place or a New Way
 We sought to perceive the flow of energy
  through each new possibility
   and how much was enough
   and how much was too much

UNTIL AT LAST
 Someone would rise
  and ask the old, old question
   to remind us of things
    we do not yet see clearly enough to remember

"TELL ME NOW MY BROTHERS
TELL ME NOW MY SISTERS
WHO SPEAKS FOR WOLF?"

And so Grandfather's Song ended . . . and my father's voice grew still.

"Did the boy learn to sing with Wolf?" I asked.

"All may," my father answered.

"And did the People always remember to ask Wolf's Question?"

My father smiled. "They remembered for a long time . . . a long time. And when the wooden ships came, bringing a new People, they looked at them and saw that what we accomplish by much thought and considering the needs of all, they accomplish by building tools and changing the Earth, with much thought of winter and little of tomorrow. We could not teach them to ask Wolf's question. They did not understand he was their brother. We knew how long it had taken us to listen to Wolf's voice. It seemed to us that These Ones could also learn. And so we cherished them . . . when we could . . . and held them off . . . when we must . . . and gave them time to learn."

"Will they learn, do you think, my father? Will they learn?"

"Sometimes wisdom comes only after great foolishness. We still hope they will learn. I do not know even

if our own People still ask their question. I only know
that at the last Great Council when we talked about the
Small Ones in their wooden ships and decided that their
way and our way might exist side by side — and decided,
therefore, to let them live . . . I only know that someone
rose to remind them of the things we had not yet learned
about these Pale Ones."

"He rose and he reminded us of what we had already learned, of how these New Ones believed that only one way was Right and all others Wrong. He wondered out loud whether they would be as patient with us — once they were strong — as we were now with them. He wondered what else might be true for them that we did not yet see. He wondered how all these things — seen and unseen — might affect our lives and the lives of our children's children's children. Then to remind us of the great difficulties that may arise from the simple omission of something we forgot to consider, he gazed slowly around the Council Circle and asked the ancient question:

"TELL ME NOW MY BROTHERS
TELL ME NOW MY SISTERS
WHO SPEAKS FOR WOLF?"

Weaving Wisdom From a Learning Story

When I first heard the Telling of *Wolf* from my Father, I was not yet three.

"What . . . may we learn from this?" he asked me.

In my best three-year-old parlance I answered, "Huh?"

"What do you think about when you hear this Story?"

"Ummm . . . Wuff!"

"Umm-hum . . . and what else?"

"Ummm . . . I dunno."

"Well," he replied with the beginnings of that infinite patience I came to value, "If you think of anything else . . . I'd like to hear about it."

So I thought about it. Wondered what learning was. Wondered what I might learn.

Finally, I decided I didn't really know the answer to either of these questions I asked myself. I decided I had to experience this Telling again — or I would never learn these answers.

I went to my Father and began the first of my endless and repeated petitions. "Daddy . . . Wuff again?"

And he began the song.

Over the years, again and again I asked to hear one of the Tellings, so that I might learn. He shared them with me one more time . . . and then asked the ancient question.

When I learned the last lesson he was able to identify in *Wolf* I was 17 years old.

During these same years, he began to share with me the nature of symbolic learning, that which transcends the immediately logical.

And at last I began to understand how much a true Learning Story might convey . . and in what manner.

So that you may witness on these pages some of the nature of my learning from my Father — what he said, what I answered — I have written down my memory of one of these exchanges . . . which took place *long* after the age of three.

"What may we learn from this?" my Father was asking, beginning the long dance between those who seek and those who beckon.

I looked up in surprise.

"This is a Learning Story?" I asked, startled, for where were the symbols of a broader reality?

"All Tellings may be learned from" he encouraged. "But surely for the People to have kept this one so long, it must contain some wisdom . . . . What do you see here?"

Searching the air for symbols finally I ventured, "Wolf, of course, and Fire . . . and Moon and Forest. Grandfather is witness to it all . . . and to the Boy's learning."

"Is Wolf not also witness?"

"Wolf is there to understand Fire . . . as Moon-Looking-Wolf seeks to understand Moon. Wolf-Looks-at-Fire does not seek to understand the People."

"Does not?" my Father asked.

But I understood his meaning. "He seeks to understand his relationship to Fire and the nature of Fire. Moon-Looking-Wolf seeks to understand the nature of Moon and many join her in her search, understanding thereby their relation to each other, understanding the People we call Wolf."

My father was pleased. His expression barely changed, but I felt his pleasure. His eyes turned to questions and I knew there was more to learn.

I thought of Moon and Wolf and Fire and saw at last the connection.

"Within the Circle of the People I see a form which has three sides. Wolf-Fire-Wolf," I described in the air, "Wolf-Fire-Boy. Each reaches out toward the other. Wolf and Boy seek understanding of Fire, are warmed by the nature of Fire. Each sees in the other's face a reflection of the nature of Fire and find between them a common curiosity.

"Other Wolf Persons explore the nature of Moon, see in her face a reflection of the reality that lies beyond." I paused and searched the images in my mind, each forming one point of the three-sided forms contained within the Circle of the People. I saw the fire in the reality which lies beyond. I saw Wolf . . and Wolf . . and Wolf regarding Moon. I saw Earth and Moon, both regarding that distant fire, both reflecting its warmth, and felt that same warmth on my face.

"We regard the Central Fire as our source of warmth, our common Center. Pulling us toward it, it encourages us toward each other."

"Is it any different for Wolf? That same Fire, that same reflection, arouses our desire to understand, to absorb within our being the reality of Fire, its nature, its flowing through Universe."

"No different," I said. "It is our nature to understand the Reality that lies beyond by watching its reflection in our Brother's face. And so, seeking understanding, Wolf and Boy are also brothers.

"Well, I will continue to consider the nature of Wolf and Boy and Fire. Of Grandfather and his quiet Joy in watching the reflection of understanding on the face of He of Eight Winters.

"I see that this is the foundation of the nature of the understanding of the People, a three-sided form within its circle, many three-sided forms, Person and Person, the Reality they regard, their relationship with each other."

I heard the Joy in my Father's voice.

"You understand the tap root of the meaning that our symbols touch, my Daughter. Do not let this understanding slip away!"

And so I sat for awhile, looking at Wolf and Moon, Boy and Grandfather, and always beyond some Central Fire.

Without moving, I danced circles around this Fire . . . and

understood all three-sided forms, all Circles however large, however small, for such is the nature of understanding. Between fire spark and starshine a difference in size, no difference in nature.

I danced the patterns into my mind, remembering them as shapes against which to measure all future understanding. Turning and circling, treading now the arched path that contains the understanding, now the straight path of Perception, I danced to the beat of the Universe, danced to the tune of one Generation caring that the next may learn, danced to my Father's love flowing through me into the Future.

"Hey ya, Ya yo!" I intoned at last, in recognition of Spirit and of the Spirit Path.

"Hey ya, Ya yo, Hoy!" My Father replied, reinforcing with his heart my growing perception.

"We dance upon the Spirit path," he said, "understanding our own direction, understanding the spinning motion of all things, circles that are lines, lines that are circles."

We sang on and on until we were exhausted. Then sat, breathing slowly, until Spirit returned to sit within its Earth Center. And we looked . . . from one to the other, to the Central Fire we never lit, which was always there, and understood the nature of our mutual caring.

At last, I raised my head again and suggested, "There is more to be learned from this Telling, my Father. I see how the People gather around their Central Fire to reach mutual understanding. I see the relationship of different Peoples and the Earth they stand on, the limits and the largeness of Space, of Time . . ." I hesitated. My patterns in the air ceased their flow.

"I shall begin again," my Father offered . . . nothing but patience filled his voice.

He paused, drumming with his fingers on his knee, keeping the rhythm of the ancient chant.

"Almost at the edge of the Circle of light cast by Central Fire, Wolf was standing . . ."

Central Fire

For those who understand the meaning of the Central Fire, there can be no explanation. For those who not yet see the mounting flames calling the hunter from his forest, the farmer from her field, gathering the People to share their wisdom toward a shared decision . . . know that each Council Fire was lit as a beacon, forming the center toward which all faced. No one of the People was the Fire. Yet the Fire was their Center, their gathered energy mounting skyward, like their prayers, toward the Reality which lies beyond.

This shared focus was constructed by many hands, like the Long Houses in which they lived. To this beacon each one brought some wood, like food to the Central Feast. Out of unity some greater purpose. What is impossible for one, many may yet accomplish.

Even in a summer's warmth, even in a small dwelling where any fire at all would have been intolerable, the Central Fire was still there . . . built by each hand, lit by the mind, by the heart, if not by any hand.

Like the Central Fire around which my Father and I always sat, fed by both hands, lit only by the heart, our Spirit dwelling, our round house, a white clapboard garage in a County that did not allow fire. Our expanding world a Circle of Two.

So did the Circle of the People face toward their Council Fire, lit whenever there was need, lit also at regular intervals to remind them of the continuing need for consensus, for unity of purpose. Individuality stood around the Council Circle, yet unity grew and changed in the Circle's Center, like the flames of the Council Fire.

"Let all leave behind their individual concerns, safe beyond the Circle. Let our thoughts draw toward our Center. Let us be warmed by our Common Purpose," some Elder would intone.

And so it was. I and you may differ, may fall to blows between us. Yet, if our thoughts turn toward the Center, I and you — and as many others as there may be — may yet build our Central Fire, create and sustain its energy, recognize our Common Purpose.

Let it be so.

This delicate strength,
With the breath
Of an almost invisible wind,
Lifts Eagle
Far beyond sight.

Paula Underwood
August 1983

The Author

Paula Underwood wrote *Who Speaks for Wolf* as a gift for all Earth's children. An oral historian, her lifelong training in an ancient Native American methodology has uniquely prepared her to share these histories with us. In addition to her writing, she is a trainer and consultant whose work in cross-cultural understanding is also based on decades of professional experience in International Communications.

Paula won the Thomas Jefferson Cup for quality writing, and is Director of *The Past is Prologue* Educational Program which was granted "Exemplary Educational Program" status by the U.S. Department of Education. In addition to creating learning experiences for educators and their students, she has developed training programs for corporate executives.

Paula has served as liaison between the Institute of Noetic Sciences and the Worldwide Indigenous Science Network. The Network is designed to help reclaim ancient knowledge, to engender respect for its wisdom, and to encourage a dialogue between Indigenous sciences and Western science. Now she increasingly works with Learning organizations — schools and corporations — as well as an expanded network of Learners.

Paula Underwood was born in Los Angeles and after 35 years in Washington, DC, lives now near San Francisco.

The Artist

Frank Howell, one of America's most highly collected artists, is best known for his intricately-detailed renderings of American Indians. He views these works as universal symbols — as a kind of visual mythology.

Reared and educated in the Midwest, Howell has been painting for over thirty years, and in addition to his acrylics and oils, is well known for his lithographs, monotypes, watercolors, drawings, and sculpture. He has taught on both highschool and college levels, has written several books, and has illustrated many others.

Frank Howell lives and works in Santa Fe, New Mexico, and his work may be seen in galleries there and throughout the United States.